PLACE
STAMP
HERE

Color Your World with Good Intentions

HUMILITY

PLACE STAMP HERE

Color Your World with Good Intentions

PLACE
STAMP
HERE

Color Your World with Good Intentions

PLACE
STAMP
HERE

Color Your World with Good Intentions

PLACE
STAMP
HERE

Color Your World with Good Intentions

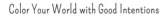
Color Your World with Good Intentions

PLACE
STAMP
HERE

ENLIGHTENMENT

PLACE
STAMP
HERE

Color Your World with Good Intentions

PLACE
STAMP
HERE

Color Your World with Good Intentions

PLACE
STAMP
HERE

Color Your World with Good Intentions

consciousness

PLACE
STAMP
HERE

Color Your World with Good Intentions

PLACE
STAMP
HERE

Color Your World with Good Intentions

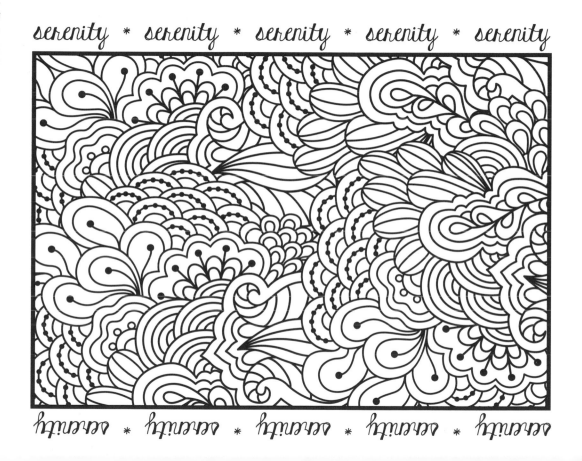

PLACE
STAMP
HERE

Color Your World with Good Intentions

PLACE
STAMP
HERE

Color Your World with Good Intentions

PLACE
STAMP
HERE

Color Your World with Good Intentions

PLACE
STAMP
HERE

Color Your World with Good Intentions

PLACE
STAMP
HERE

Color Your World with Good Intentions

PLACE
STAMP
HERE

Color Your World with Good Intentions

PLACE
STAMP
HERE

Color Your World with Good Intentions

PLACE
STAMP
HERE

Color Your World with Good Intentions

PLACE
STAMP
HERE

Color Your World with Good Intentions